Robin Hood

Story written by Gill Munton
Illustrated by Tim Archbold

Speed Sounds

Consonants *Ask children to say the sounds.*

f ff ph	l ll (le)	m mm	n nn kn	r (rr) wr	s ss se ce	v (ve)	z zz se s	sh	th	ng nk

b bb	c k ck	d dd	g gg	h	j g ge	p pp	qu	t tt	w (wh)	x	y	ch tch

Each box contains one sound but sometimes more than one grapheme.
*Focus graphemes for this story are **circled**.*

4

Vowels

Ask children to say the sounds in and out of order.

a	e	i	o	u	ay	ee	igh	ow
	ea					y	i	o
at	hen	in	on	up	day	see	high	blow

oo		ar	or	air	ir	ou	oy
			oor				oi
			ore				
zoo	look	car	for	fair	whirl	shout	boy

Story Green Words

Ask children to read the words first in Fred Talk and then say the word.

Robin Hood   band of Merry Men   John* Little   poor   crook
brags   sprang   strength*   bridge*   rooks   brook

Ask children to say the syllables and then read the whole word.

con|test   a|rrow

Ask children to read the root first and then the whole word with the suffix.

grunt → grunted   gasp → gasped   whack → whacked

happen → happened

* Challenge Words

6

Vocabulary Check

Discuss the meaning (as used in the story) after the children have read each word.

	definition:	sentence:
band of Merry Men	*Robin Hood's gang*	*Robin Hood lived in the woods with his band of Merry Men.*
crook	*a robber*	*To the rich he was a crook …*
brags	*shows off*	*John Little brags that he can win …*
contest	*a fight*	*a contest with Robin Hood.*
fast-running brook	*a little river where water runs very quickly*	*He stepped on to the wooden bridge which crossed the fast-running brook.*
still	*not move*	*Both men stood very still.*

Red Words

Ask children to practise reading the words across the rows, down the columns and in and out of order clearly and quickly.

your	who	tall	you
of	to	want	they
said	call	all	one
was	are	your	do
want	some	who	school

Robin Hood

As the storybooks will tell you,
Robin Hood lived in the woods
with his band of Merry Men,
robbing from the rich and giving to the poor.
To the rich he was a crook,
but to the poor that he helped,
he was a good man.

In this story, a man called John Little
brags that he can win a contest with Robin Hood.

"I am going hunting," Robin said to his
Merry Men. "I will not be long."

He stepped on to the wooden bridge
which crossed the fast-running brook.

On the bridge he met a man,
tall, and strong-looking.
(This was John Little.)

Both men stood very still.

Then Robin said, "Let me get past, will you?"

"I will not," grunted John.

"Then I will shoot an arrow at your chest!"
Robin took an arrow from his belt.

John shook his head.
"I have only a stick in my hand," he said.
"I don't mind having a contest, but you must
put that arrow back and find a stick.
Then I will set upon you, and I will win!"

So Robin cut himself a stick.
He swung it at John Little, and then sprang at him,
hitting John with his stick.

John gasped, and whacked Robin
with all his strength.
Robin fell off the bridge and into
the brook!

Both men began to grin. John stood on the bridge
and Robin stood up to his neck in the brook.

John hooked him out by the foot
with his stick,
and then Robin, wet to the skin,
called to his Merry Men.

When Robin told them what had happened,
the Merry Men wanted to push John into the brook.

But Robin said, "A man who can win a contest with me is a good
man to have for a pal.
John Little, you can be
one of my Merry Men,
and as you are so big
and tall, we shall call you
Little John!"

As they went back to the camp,
they shot ten rooks and took ten fish from the brook.
So Robin Hood and all his Merry Men had a very good lunch,
cooked by Little John!

Questions to talk about

Ask children to TTYP each question using 'Fastest finger' (FF) or 'Have a think' (HaT).

p.9 (FF) Who wanted a contest with Robin Hood?

p.10 (FF) How did Robin try to cross the fast-running brook?

p.11 (FF) What does Robin threaten to do if John will not let him pass?

p.12 (FF) What happened when John whacked Robin with all his strength?

p.13 (FF) How did John Little help Robin out of the brook?

p.14 (HaT) Why did Robin disagree with his Merry Men?

p.15 (FF) Who cooked lunch for the Merry Men?

Questions to read and answer

(Children complete without your help.)

1. Where did Robin Hood live?
   Robin Hood lived **in the woods / a box / a flat**.

2. Where did John and Robin meet?
   John met Robin **on a bridge / in a stream / in a wood**.

3. How did John hook Robin out of the brook?
   John hooked Robin out of the brook by **the chest / foot / hand**.

4. Where did the Merry Men want to push John?
   The Merry Men wanted to push John into **the mud / sand / brook**.

5. What did Little John cook for lunch?
   Lunch was **ten rooks and ten fish / ten chickens and ten eggs / ten apples and ten fish**.

Speedy Green Words

lived	giving	story	mind
foot	told	took	which
head	out	little	good
looking	still	that	helped
himself	crossed	stick	took

Contents

Extremes of weather

Weather is the effect of changes in the atmosphere on the land and sea. Weather varies every day, from moment to moment. We usually know what kind of weather to expect in a particular season, but sometimes the weather becomes extreme and wild.

▼ *Many Burmese people lost everything in the devastating storm that hit Myanmar in May 2008.*

Bad weather

Weather can suddenly bring freak events which are unusual for the time of year and the region. These can include violent hurricanes, whirling tornadoes and sudden heavy outbursts of rain. These events are becoming more frequent and even more extreme. Human activity may be making planet Earth warmer. We call this **global warming**. Most scientists believe global warming is responsible for the increase in extreme weather.

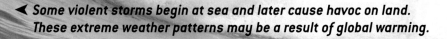

◄ *Some violent storms begin at sea and later cause havoc on land. These extreme weather patterns may be a result of global warming.*

CASE STUDY

Cyclone Nargis

On 2 May, 2008, winds that had started in south-east India hurled into the country of Myanmar (previously known as Burma), reaching speeds of over 165 km per hour. Over a few days, thousands of people were killed in the rushing winds and surging seas of the **cyclone**. During the following weeks, many more Burmese people were killed and at least 2 million were affected by the flooding and food shortages.

The Irrawaddy Delta (a delta is a landform at the mouth of a river) was worst hit as the wind whipped up a huge wall of water that reached 40 km inland. The delta was once home to **mangrove forests**. These forests of tangled roots were once a natural barrier against the storms. However, many of the mangrove forests had been cleared to make way for shrimp farms and rice paddies.

Entire villages were swallowed up in the raging waters and winds. There was no defence and nowhere for people to flee as the waters surged inland.

Power lines came down. Roads and bridges were flattened and collapsed. Seawater destroyed fresh water supplies. Survivors were homeless and hungry, reliant on foreign aid workers for food. They lost their livelihoods and many family members. Diseases such as cholera spread with dirty water. Months and years after Cyclone Nargis, people will continue to suffer.

"If you look at the path of the cyclone that hit Myanmar, it hit exactly where it was going to do the most damage, and it's doing the most damage because much of the protective vegetation was cleared."

Jeff NcNeely, chief scientist for the International Union for the Conservation of Nature

▼ *It may take several years to rebuild villages and towns in parts of the Irrawaddy Delta.*

The world of weather

Most people know roughly what type of weather to expect in a particular season in a certain region. This pattern of weather is the climate. The climate depends on a region's distance from sea, its altitude (the height above sea level) and its position from the equator (an imaginary line drawn around the middle of the world). Areas near the equator are nearer the sun and receive more warmth.

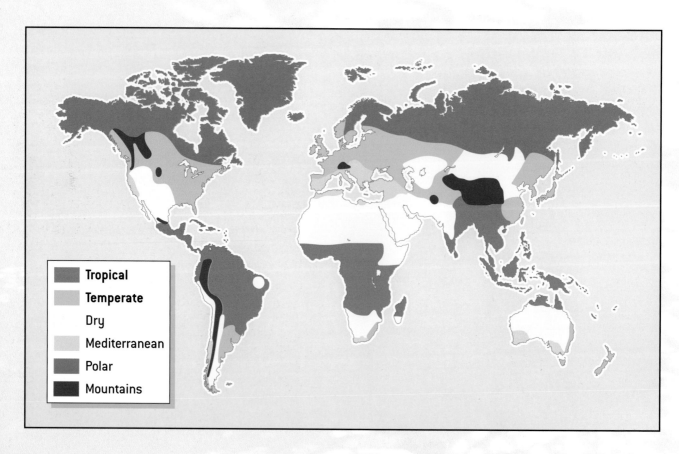

Tropical
Temperate
Dry
Mediterranean
Polar
Mountains

▲ *This map shows the different climate zones around the world.*

6

If faced with periods of prolonged ➤ drought, farmers will find it hard to grow their normal crops.

Living with the weather

Climate influences the features of the landscape, what farmers can grow, where people live and the type of houses they build. People living in Australia expect hot, dry weather. They grow crops that thrive in the warm sunshine. People in Russia know how to keep warm during the freezing winters because they are so used to them. Around the world people have adapted to the stable weather patterns of a climate.

But what happens when the climate changes abruptly and dramatically – when the changes are not part of a natural process of change but created by human activity? The result is climate chaos.

CASE STUDY

The greenhouse effect

Gases high in the atmosphere, such as carbon dioxide (CO_2), act as an invisible blanket around Earth. They stop heat escaping into space at night.

They work just like glass in a greenhouse, so this is called the 'greenhouse effect'. It keeps the planet at the right temperature for plants, animals and humans to live. However, humans are adding many more 'greenhouse gases' such as carbon dioxide into the atmosphere. The result is that the blanket is working too well, and the planet is warming up. This is global warming, and it is making big changes to our climate.

◄ *We are experiencing more frequent unusual weather events, probably due to changes in the climate.*

Climate change

Since the beginning of life on Earth there has been **climate change**. Climates have changed slowly over thousands of years. There have been ice ages when much of the planet was covered with ice.

Climates in the past

Evidence from past climates is found in **ice cores** (samples) taken from the North and South Poles and sediments deep in the ocean floor. Scientists have evidence today that the world's climate is changing more rapidly and more seriously than it has ever done before. Many people believe that the changes will be chaotic and catastrophic.

"Levels of greenhouse gases continue to rise in the atmosphere and the rate of that rise is accelerating. We are already seeing the impacts of climate change and the scale of those impacts will also accelerate, until we decide to do something about it."

Martin Parry, co-chair of the IPCC (Intergovernmental Panel of Climate Change)

What are the causes?

Most of the **energy** we use, from petrol for cars to electricity for a computer, comes from burning **fossil fuels** in power stations. These fossil fuels include coal, oil and gas. A large amount of carbon dioxide is released when oil and coal are burned. A certain amount of carbon dioxide in the atmosphere naturally keeps the Earth's temperature in balance. But too much carbon dioxide traps too much heat, causing global warming and climate change.

Effects of climate change

Warmer temperatures in the world have far-reaching effects, from land to sea. They are causing more frequent and stronger extreme weather events such as heatwaves, storms, torrential rain, raging winds and hurricanes.

▲ *Many office lights blaze with energy all night in the world's major cities.*

◄ *There have been more instances of major forest fires in many countries around the world in recent years.*

WHAT CAN BE DONE?

The climate is changing in ways that no one could have predicted. We cannot control the natural changes and processes of the climate but we can control what we do on Earth. We know what is causing climate change. Are we prepared to adapt our lifestyles, such as using cars and aeroplanes less frequently, to prevent climate change from spiralling out of control?

The big melt

Since the beginning of the 20th century the average surface temperature on Earth has risen by 0.74°C. This may not sound very much, but even a small change can make an enormous difference to the world's climate. The world just keeps on getting warmer.

Warming Arctic

The ice around the poles formed over millions of years. Each year some ice melts from the ice caps, but is replaced by more ice during the freezing Arctic winters. Warmer temperatures are melting ice more quickly. Many scientists predict floating sea ice will disappear from the North Pole – perhaps as early as the year 2080.

Ice reflects heat back to the sun. Without ice, more heat will be absorbed into the Earth's atmosphere, raising temperatures around the world.

Windy waters

The oceans make up a liquid part of a global system that influences the world's climate. Seawater moves around the world constantly, a little like a conveyor belt. Winds, the water's temperature, its salinity (how salty it is) keep the fluid conveyor belt moving – cold, salty water is denser (heavier) than warm water so it sinks down, dragging in warmer water behind it. More freshwater coming from melting glaciers in the poles could change the balance of the ocean conveyor belt.

▼ *Sea levels are rising as ice caps melt into the oceans because of global warming.*

Flooded by the sea

Warmer water takes up more room than cooler water, making the sea level rise. This is a dangerous threat for low-level coastal countries and regions such as Florida, Bangladesh and the Netherlands. It could get a lot worse, too – if all the ice in the Arctic and Antarctic melted, the meltwater could raise sea levels by at least another 12 m worldwide.

▲ *Melting glaciers could change ocean currents – with drastic results.*

Melting ground

Permafrost, or permanently frozen ground, stretches from Siberia to Alaska. Studies show it is warming up. Melting permafrost destroys roads and buildings built on the frozen ground. It could also release a greenhouse gas called methane locked underground. With more methane in the atmosphere, the atmosphere will heat up.

CASE STUDY

Bangladesh floods

Bangladesh is one of the poorest countries in the world. It is vulnerable to flooding. More than 50 rivers flow into the country, most of which is less than 12 m above sea level. Every year, monsoon rains, cyclones and rising rivers flood parts of the country. But in 1998, severe flooding killed more than 1,000 people. Millions were made homeless and 2 million tonnes of rice crops were ruined. Floods were caused by the effect of high meltwater from the Himalayas and lengthy monsoon rains swelling the rivers. If sea levels continue to rise, the effects on a country such as Bangladesh could be catastrophic.

As severe flooding hits Bangladesh, citizens try ➤ *to move their possessions to higher ground.*

Deadly hurricanes

Wild winds and storms can batter land. They move at such speed that they destroy everything in their path. Storms with winds of more than 120 km per hour are called hurricanes, cyclones and typhoons. These violent spinning storms bring clouds, wild winds and heavy rains. They are one of nature's deadliest forces.

The making of a hurricane

Hurricanes form in tropical climates over very warm seas. The wind and clouds rise quickly and start to spin. The spinning wind makes the hurricane move even more quickly. A hurricane can start with winds churning up the warm waves. Over a few days, the storm picks up energy.

▼ *Storm surges form as winds whip up huge waves that batter the coast.*

column of air that sweeps across land. It is usually small – but deadly. The wind pressure can make buildings collapse. Houses, people and cars are lifted up in the funnel of wind. The tornado forms at the base of a thundercloud (often after a hurricane) as a strong up current of warm air starts to spin. Strong air sucks in air from below. The highest wind speeds happen inside tornadoes.

The hurricane increases as it travels towards land. The centre of the storm is called an eye. Here, the skies are clear and the temperatures high. The winds that surround the eye are the strongest and most dangerous. Hurricanes suck up water from the ocean surface which turns to vapour. The hurricane winds cool near land, and the water vapour turns to heavy rain.

As a hurricane reaches land, it whips up a massive wall of seawater called a storm surge. This causes the most devastation to the coastline.

Spinning tornadoes

Exploding houses, flying cars – this is the effect of a tornado, sometimes called a twister. This is a whizzing, spinning

Fact bank

- Cyclone Nargis, Myanmar, 2008 – 140,000 dead or missing.

- Hurricane Katrina, United States, 2005 – at least 1,800 dead.

- Orissa cyclone, Northern India, 1999 – at least 10,000 dead.

- Hurricane Mitch, Central America, 1998 – at least 11,000 dead.

- Tropical Storm Thelma, Philippines, 1991 – 6,000 dead.

- Bangladesh cyclone, Bangladesh, 1991 – about 138,000 dead.

- Bhola cyclone, (East Pakistan, now Bangladesh), 1970 – at least 300,000 dead.

Drying up

While some regions in the world are flooding more due to climate change, other countries such as Australia and Africa are getting too little rain and too much heat. Cracks open up in the dry, scorched earth. Animals scrape around in the heat for any plants to eat. When there is too little rainfall over a long period, drought occurs.

Managing drought

Drought cannot be prevented, but people are still able to manage the hot, dry conditions. Planting trees helps store water in their trunks, then their leaves slowly release moisture back into the air. Fences made from rows of trees can help stop **desertification**. Planting crops that need little water, such as **cassava**, helps provide people with food during a time of drought.

Getting fresh water

Some countries try to solve their water shortages by turning salty water from the sea into fresh drinking water in a process called desalination.

◄ *Once one of the largest inland seas, much of the Aral Sea has now dried up.*

However, this uses up lots of energy and is so costly that many countries cannot afford it. Irrigation systems can channel water from rivers and lakes to where it is needed. However, if too much freshwater is diverted, the rivers and lakes are likely to dry up completely.

Desalination plants, such as this one in ➤ Australia, are always situated close to the sea.

CASE STUDY

Australian drought

Australia is a country used to long hot summers and even droughts. However, since 2003, parts of the country have been experiencing the worst and longest drought for 100 years, with severe water shortages. Nearly half of Australia's farming produce comes from the Murray-Darling Basin but the two rivers that feed the area are drying up. There is no water to feed crops or animals. Crops, such as wheat and rice, are failing. This means that prices of wheat and rice rise in other parts of the world, too, and there is a shortage of these basic foods. Around the world, others feel the effect of the Australian drought because the price of rice or bread has risen so high.

According to one report Australia is likely to experience severe droughts twice as often, because of climate change. Yet Australia continues to release more carbon dioxide into the atmosphere than most other countries of the world.

◄ Large areas of land in Australia that were once covered in river water are now just parched ground.

Flood alert

Surging seas driven by winds quickly flood the coast. Heavy downpours of rain flood inland areas. Houses wash away, fields are swamped with water and crops are destroyed, while drains burst allowing sewage to run freely. Floods also kill. They cause devastation and misery long after the waters have dried up.

Bursting banks

The land usually soaks up rainfall rather like a sponge soaks up water. The water runs underground back into rivers and then the seas. But when too much rain falls too quickly, the land cannot soak it up. Rivers swell with water and burst their banks. Fierce winds hurl waves of seawater over the land, too.

Landslides

In hilly areas, heavy rains bring the threat of landslides. Rocks and soil underground become **sodden** and loose. The ground collapses beneath them, tumbling down slopes. Sometimes, the force of the slide uproots houses and trees, with devastating effect.

◄ *Sudden floods can occur in temperate climates and in hot climates. They cause huge damage and take a lot of cleaning up.*

▲ *Farmers in rice paddy fields in hot climates rely on the monsoon rains.*

Monsoon rains

Every summer, southern Asia and especially India, is drenched for several months by seasonal heavy rains, called monsoons. These are carried in moist air masses that move from the Indian Ocean to the south. The monsoon is crucial to farmers in the region. Crops wither if there is too little monsoon rain; they wash away if the rains are too heavy. Forecasting the arrival of monsoons is critical – farmers need to know when the monsoons are coming so that they can plant crops to take advantage of the rains.

Heavy rainfall can ➤ *have a devastating effect if people are unprepared for the downpour.*

WHAT CAN BE DONE?

Flood plains (flat areas along rivers that flood if water levels rise) ditches, ponds and marshes store and slowly release floodwaters. However, in some parts of the world such as England, people continue to build on flood plains. Flood defences set up to prevent flooding on the built-up flood plains can cause even greater problems. Without the natural protection of the flood plains, flooding further downstream can become very severe. Leaving these natural features in place reduces the risk of the spread of flooding. For example, the flood plains of the River Morova in the Slovak Republic absorbed much water when the River Danube flooded in 2002 – and protected Bratislava from higher flooding levels.

El Niño and his sister

Scientists first identified a weather pattern they called El Niño in the warm waters of the Pacific Ocean in the 1970s. They believe that it has been a feature of the climate for the last 15,000 years, but they fear its effects could get worse because of climate change. El Niño means 'the little boy' in Spanish.

All about El Niño

Usually, winds called trade winds drive the warm surface waters of the Pacific Ocean from the west towards the east. The wind gathers water as it passes over the ocean, and this falls as rain over Indonesia and Australia. Because the wind is blowing away from the coast of South America, it leaves that region very dry. Off the coast of South America, cold water rises from the deep ocean to replace the warm water that the winds have pushed away. This carries lots of nutrients to the surface. These help feed huge populations of fish, which local people catch for food.

However, every two to seven years, this weather pattern is turned around. The trade winds reverse, and blow from east to west. Warm water then flows eastwards towards the coast of South America.

This map shows ➤ how trade winds change during the weather pattern known as El Niño.

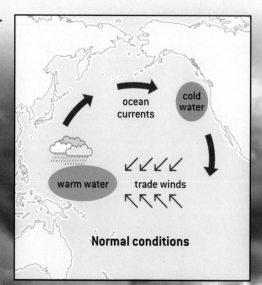

Normal conditions

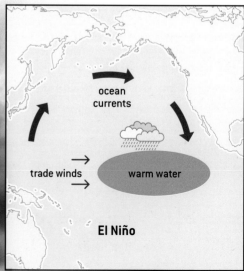

El Niño

▲ *Peruvian villagers try to cope with a landslide caused by El Niño.*

The result of El Niño is warmer, wetter weather around South America, causing floods even in the Caribbean and southern United States. Without warm waters that turn to rain there is drought over Indonesia and Australasia in the western Pacific. There can also be storms in places like Hawaii.

Warm water off South America blocks rising cold water from the deep ocean. There are fewer nutrients in the seawater, so fish numbers drop. There is nothing for fishing boats or seabirds to catch, and birds and some people starve.

La Niña

El Niño is often followed by its little sister, La Niña. As trade winds pick up force again, they drag more warm water away in the west Pacific, leaving behind a spread of colder waters. Heavy rains fall in the west while it is dry in the east Pacific, with hurricanes in the Atlantic.

Scientists know that changes to the air and water in the Pacific have a knock-on effect around the world. The strongest El Niño in 1997–98 coincided with very heavy rains. There were floods in south-east Africa, and great storms in the United States and the Caribbean.

19

Changing landscape

Over thousands of years, the weather shapes the land, carving out valleys, building up sandbanks, **eroding** hills. Extreme weather can reshape land in hours, too. Fierce rains can cause masses of sodden earth to tumble down a mountain. Waves churned up by winds and warm weather hurl rocks or soil over coastlines.

Dust storms

Sandstorms can rapidly change the appearance of an area with the shifting and re-forming of dunes by the wind. Dust storms form when strong winds lift dust into the air. The winds carry tonnes of dust overland. Dust from storms in the Sahara desert, North Africa, can fall as far away as Greenland and the United States.

Chopped away

Cutting down forests is called **deforestation**. This has a dramatic effect upon the health of the soil and on the way that the land copes with different weather conditions. Tree roots drink up water and trap water in the soil. Without trees, the land is eroded and floods more easily.

Cutting down ➤ *forests can cause land to flood when rain falls heavily.*

CASE STUDY

Amazon forest

The Amazon rainforest is one of the most **ecologically** diverse areas on Earth. The full extent of the biodiversity (range of life) in the towering trees, the snaking rivers and the carpets of plants is still not known, and there are millions of different species in the Amazon rainforest yet to be identified.

A drought in 2005 left fish stranded in dry rivers. Fires caused by the build-up of heat blasted through the thick forest, destroying vast tracts of it.

Scientists believe the drought and continuing dry weather in this region is partly caused by climate change. It is also linked directly to human activity. Large areas of the forest have been cut down to make way for crop land or to provide timber to sell. The combined effect is to push the Amazon environment towards tipping point – a point from which it will not recover. The loss of tree cover will increase the levels of carbon dioxide in the atmosphere and global warming will continue to get worse.

"The Amazon is facing threats on two fronts – climate change and direct deforestation.... Reducing further deforestation could slow global warming, maintain rainfall and conserve biodiversity."

Dr Richard Betts, Met Office climate scientist, 2007

➤ There is a wonderful natural diversity of life at all levels in the Amazon rainforest.

Life in danger

The **ecosystems** of all living plants and animals are linked to climate and weather. Sudden changes in the climate or recurrent extreme weather events have a major effect on Earth's biodiversity. It can affect a species' migration patterns, feeding habits and habitats. It can threaten some species with extinction.

▼ *Today, the Emperor penguin has less available food due to climate change.*

CASE STUDY

Disappearing habitats

Over the last 50 years, the number of Emperor penguins living in western Antarctica has halved. An unusually warm spell of weather in the late 1970s reduced the amount of ice floating on the sea. This meant there were far fewer krill, tiny creatures that live under the ice and on which the penguins feed. As a result, many Emperor penguin chicks starved to death.

Siberian cranes breed in Russia and Siberia and then migrate to China. The cranes like to breed in the wide open spaces of the **Arctic tundra** and **taiga**. The Arctic permafrost limits tree growth, but as the ground begins to warm up, trees grow quickly, altering the cranes' habitat.

Changing ecosystems

The Tibetan Plateau is 4,500 m above ground level and four times the size of France (2.5 million square km). It is often called the 'roof of the world'. Grassy plains, icy blue lakes, hot deserts and thick forests stretch along the plateau. Endangered animals such as the Tibetan antelope have adapted to the icy, harsh winters. But higher temperatures have far-reaching effects on the fragile ecosystem. Warmer summers mean there is less grass for native animals such as yaks. More sheep and cattle graze during the longer summer – overgrazing damages the soil and threatens the existence of many unique plant species. Surface water **evaporates** more quickly, leading to a drop in water levels in the rivers. This threatens the water supply of the local people and speeds up the process of desertification.

More than half of the world's ▼
estimated 10 million species of plants and animals live in tropical rainforest, such as the Amazon rainforest.

▲ *The golden toad has not been seen for over 20 years and is probably extinct.*

Dead and gone

The only known population of golden toad (*Bufo periglenes*), from the Monteverde cloud forest, of Costa Rica, has not been seen since 1989 after low rainfall and high temperatures during El Niño. The toad may be the first known animal to disappear as a result of global warming.

The human impact

Climate change threatens the well being of people across the world, especially those in less economically developed countries. These countries are often without the resources to build elaborate flood defences or to set up complex irrigation or desalination systems.

How will we cope?

Extreme weather events cause enormous problems, even when they are rare, but what will we do as they become more common and more unpredictable?

> "Climate change threatens the basic elements of life for people around the world – access to water, food, health and the use of land and the environment."
>
> **Stern Review on the Economics of Climate Change, 2006**

▼ *This satellite image shows a swirling hurricane heading for land.*

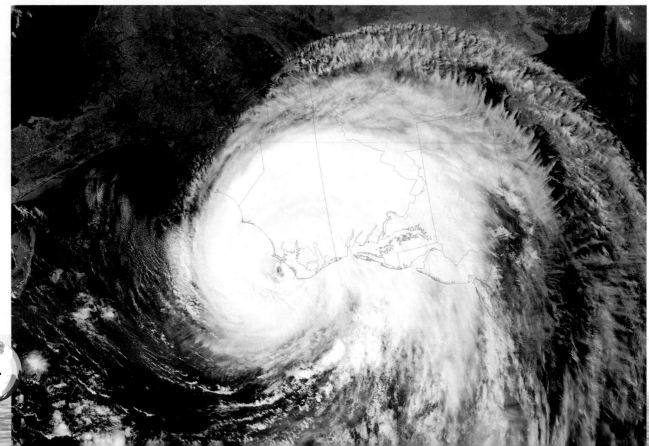

Illness

Disease spreads in floods. Mosquito-borne diseases such as malaria spread further in unusually warm weather. Droughts and floods destroy crops and homes. Shortages of food cause people to become malnourished and to die.

Forecasting

Weather forecasting saves lives. Fishing boats head for land when fierce storms build. People move to higher ground when heavy rains threaten. The less economically developed countries, often most vulnerable to extreme weather conditions, benefit particularly from accurate forecasting. Forecasts are often made using the technology of satellites or from collecting data from observations on land, sea and air.

Images from satellites show the formation and likely path of a hurricane. No one can stop a hurricane but early warnings enable people to prepare better. People stock up on fresh water, buy supplies of food and fuel, or leave.

Migration

Extreme weather conditions and warmer temperatures force people to find new land on which to farm and live. However, farming too much on land that has limited water supplies weakens the soil. It becomes dry and dusty.

▲ *Once fertile land in areas such as the Arab Emirates has become poor as a result of climate change.*

Fact bank

- An estimated 150,000 people die every year from diseases that the changing climate has encouraged to spread.

- Malaria, which currently kills up to 3 million people a year, will spread to new areas in warmer, wetter weather.

If the world temperature increases by 2°C by 2050:

- 50 million people will be forced to leave their homes.

- Acute water shortages will affect up to 3 billion people.

- 30 million more people will go hungry as crops fail.

Managing the weather

Climate change is happening, but we can take action to ensure that it does not get worse. We can protect ourselves against its worst impacts, by adapting our way of life. We can also build flood defences and conserve forests to lessen the effects of climate chaos.

Do we plan for disasters?

When engineers and architects build houses and even towns, they plan for various circumstances, including freak weather conditions. They weigh up the likelihood of floods or fierce storms and then plan accordingly, taking into account the cost of all the plans. But what level of damage do we need to plan for when the climate is so chaotic and unpredictable? The Thames Barrier in London is a flood barrier that straddles the River Thames.

It was planned when sea levels were rising at about 1.8 mm a year. Since then, the rate has nearly doubled and global warming is recognised as a reality and threat. If sea levels rise more quickly and more intensely than predicted, the barrier may not prevent flooding in London in the future.

Nature's best

Nature's own features are often the best barrier against changing conditions.

◀ *London's Thames Barrier was built between 1974 and 1984, but is it becoming out of date already?*

◄ Grassy sand dunes often provide those living by the coast with the best defence against high seas.

Making rain

In the United States, Los Angeles County officials approved a plan in 2008 to use '**cloud seeding**' methods in an attempt to improve rainfall during drought conditions. Machines spray tiny pieces of silver iodide into the atmosphere. The silver iodide mixes with clouds to make more ice crystals which may make rain fall. It is not known for certain whether this works, but officials were willing to pay US $800,000 for the trials.

As sea levels rise, the solution may be to move away from coastal areas and instead, build sand dunes and salt marshes. These provide a natural defence against incoming seas, protecting land and lives further inland.

WHAT CAN BE DONE?

The weather is packed with energy. Using this energy to provide for our energy needs avoids the need to use up fossil fuels. From the shining sun to the wind and waves, energy from the weather can be used to power the world. Harnessing energy from such **renewable** sources will reduce the amount of carbon dioxide **emissions** and prevent increased climate change and further damage to the planet.

We can harness the natural energy from the ► winds using turbines. This renewable form of energy will not harm our planet.

27

Protecting our planet

We cannot change the weather. We cannot stop natural cycles in the climate or freak weather events. We cannot completely stop climate change, but we can all take action to prevent human activity from worsening the effects of climate change.

Government action

The Kyoto Protocol, an international agreement adopted in 1997, set a maximum amount of carbon dioxide emissions that more economically developed countries could produce. It did not enter into force until 2005. The United States has not signed the agreement, and Australia only signed in 2008. The agreement is due to run out in 2012. It is clear that all nations need to play a part if we want to slow or halt climate change.

The butterfly effect

The idea that small events, such as a butterfly flapping its wings, can have far-reaching consequences, such as influencing the formation of a tornado is known as the butterfly effect.

◀ *If we reduce our carbon output, we can reduce global warming. The butterfly effect would ensure that the positive benefits of this would be felt worldwide.*

No one can prove or disprove that the movement of a butterfly's wings on the wind and atmosphere may have a knock-on effect on a tornado because the formation of a tornado is influenced by so many factors. But we do know that what happens in one part of the world makes a difference in another part. Burning fossil fuels in the United Kingdom can affect the climate many miles away in Africa where it can destroy a farmer's crop and livelihood.

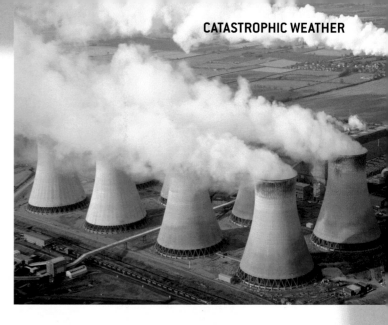

▲ *Many power stations are working to reduce gas emissions, but we all need a cleaner, greener future for energy.*

HOW CAN WE PROTECT OUR PLANET?

- Join a campaign to encourage governments to take action to use non-polluting fuels.

- Ride a bike or catch a bus or take a train instead of using a car.

- Work out, and try to reduce, your carbon footprint – this is the amount of greenhouse gas emissions we produce in our everyday life. There are several sites on the Internet which help work out a carbon footprint.

- Have a holiday in your own country. Holiday flights are a major producer of greenhouse gases.

- Recycle: using recycled material consumes less energy than using new materials.

- Reuse: buy products that can be used again. You will also save the energy used to make them, and reduce the amount of **landfill space** needed to contain the waste.

- Reduce: only buy what you need. This means there is less to throw away.

Farmers as far ➤ away as Africa will benefit if people in the United Kingdom cut carbon emissions.

Glossary

Arctic tundra area near the Poles where no trees grow because of the cold climate

cassava a tropical plant that people in South America use to make flour

climate change long-term changes in the world's weather patterns

'cloud seeding' dropping chemicals onto clouds to make it rain

cyclone any kind of severe tropical storm

deforestation chopping down huge areas of forest

desertification the spread of dry and infertile land

ecologically to do with the relationship between living things and their environment

ecosystems balance between communities of animals and plants and their environments

emissions gases or chemicals released into the atmosphere

energy power sources, such as gas, used to make things work

eroding wearing away of the land

evaporate when water turns into invisible water vapour in the air

fossil fuels fuels such as oil, coal and gas. These fuels formed from the remains of plants and animals

global warming the gradual warming of the Earth's climate

ice cores plugs of ice dug out through the depths of a glacier

landfill space areas in which huge amounts of rubbish are dumped

mangrove forests forests of mangrove trees which grow in saltwater

renewable resources which form again in a short period of time

sodden completely wet through

taiga area near the Poles, warmer than Arctic tundra, where some trees grow

temperate climate pattern that has mild winters and summers

tropical climate pattern that has very hot weather for much of the year

Further information

Books

Climate Change (21ˢᵗ Century Debates) by Simon Scoones
(Wayland, 2001)

Floods (Natural Disasters) by Chris Oxlade (Wayland, 2007)

Tsunamis (Natural Disasters) by Louise and Richard Spilsbury
(Wayland, 2007)

Global Warming (Your Environment) by Susannah Bradley
(Franklin Watts, 2008)

Weather (Earthwise) by Jim Pipe (Franklin Watts, 2008)

Climate Change (Can the Earth Cope?) by Richard Spilsbury
(Wayland, 2008)

Climate Change (The World Today) by Colin Hynson (Franklin
Watts, 2008)

Websites

Discover more about weather and how it works at:
www.bbc.co.uk/weather/weatherwise/factfiles

Learn about carbon footprints, calculate your own carbon footprint
and find out how you can reduce it at:
www.mycarbonfootprint.eu/index.cfm?language=en

Index